16-98

SEAS AND OCEANS

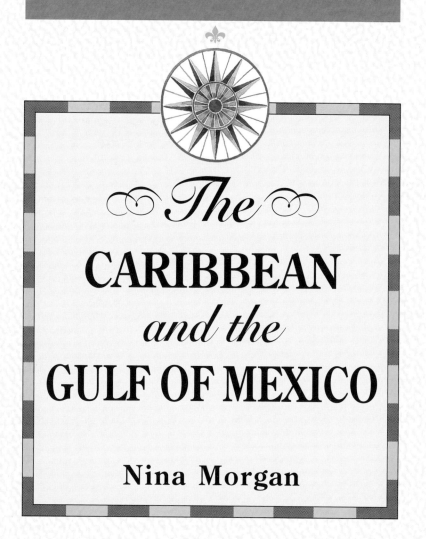

The CARIBBEAN *and the* GULF OF MEXICO

Nina Morgan

RSVP

RAINTREE
STECK-VAUGHN
PUBLISHERS
The Steck-Vaughn Company

Austin, Texas

Seas and Oceans series

The Atlantic Ocean
The Caribbean and the Gulf of Mexico
The Indian Ocean
The Mediterranean Sea
The North Sea and the Baltic Sea
The Pacific Ocean
The Polar Seas
The Red Sea and the Arabian Gulf

Cover: Caneel Bay and resort, St. John, U.S. Virgin Islands
(© Bill Ross/Westlight)

© **Copyright 1997, text, Steck-Vaughn Company**

Published by Raintree Steck-Vaughn Publishers,
an imprint of Steck-Vaughn Company

Library of Congress Cataloging-in-Publication Data
Morgan, Nina.
The Caribbean and the Gulf of Mexico / Nina Morgan.
    p.   cm.—(Seas and oceans)
    Includes bibliographical references (p.) and index.
    Summary: Covers the geography, climate, resources, and history of the Caribbean and Gulf of Mexico regions.
    ISBN 0-8172-4508-1
    1. Caribbean Area— Description and travel—Juvenile literature.
    2. Caribbean Sea—Juvenile literature.
    3. Mexico, Gulf of—Juvenile literature.
    [1. Caribbean Area. 2. Caribbean Sea. 3. Mexico, Gulf of.]
    I. Title. II. Series: Seas and oceans (Austin, Tex.)
    [F2171.3.M67   1997]
    917.29—dc20   96-8353

Printed in Italy. Bound in the United States.
1 2 3 4 5 6 7 8 9 0 0 01 00 99 98 97

Picture acknowledgments:
Dieter Betz 26–27; Ecoscene 4, 15 (Shaffer), 23 (Anthony Cooper); Eye Ubiquitous 7 (James Davis), 8–9 (L. Fordyce), 14 (Tim Page), 16 (L. Fordyce), 20–21 (James Davis), 25 (James Davis), 27 (top/David Cumming), 32 (C.M. Leask), 34 (Tim Page), 35 (James Davis), 41 (James Davis), 44 (Bruce Adams), 45 (Bruce Adams); Frank Lane Picture Agency 21 (top/Hugh Clark); Geoscience 6–7 (Dr. B. Booth), 28, 31 (top); Impact 5 (Sergio Dorantes), 39 (bottom/Sergio Dorantes); Life File 29 (Sue Davis), 30–31 (Juliet Highet), 40 (Richard Powers); Oxford Scientific Films 12 (Lawrence Gould); Panos Pictures 17 (Marc French), 39 (top/ P. Wolmuth); Papillio 22; Topham Picture Point 18, 19, 42; Wayland Picture Library 36. All artwork is supplied by Hardlines except Peter Bull 11 (top) and Stephen Chabluk 10–11 and 34–35.

Contents

Words that appear in **bold** in the text can be found in the glossary on page 46.

Contrasting Seas

The Caribbean Sea and the Gulf of Mexico are both western extensions, or arms, of the Atlantic Ocean. These two partially enclosed bodies of water are, however, very different. The differences depend on the way they were formed and the way the people who live near them make use of the natural resources each has to offer.

A mention of the Caribbean brings images of lush islands, white beaches, dramatic volcanic peaks, clear blue seas, coral **reefs**, and beautiful harbors full of small boats. In fact, tourism is the largest industry there. For many people, visiting the Caribbean is a dream vacation.

Islands dominate the geography and lifestyle in the Caribbean. The curved chain of islands that makes up the Greater and Lesser Antilles separates the Caribbean Sea from the Atlantic Ocean.

Below: In the Caribbean, islands are very important features. In the Gulf of Mexico, coastlines and surrounding large land areas dominate the geography.

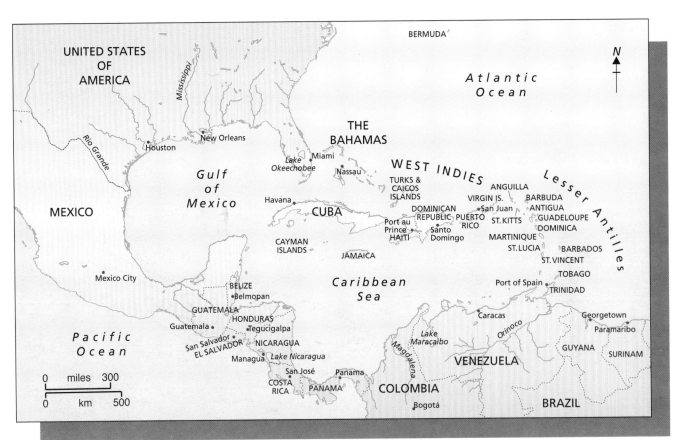

Left: The white sands and sparkling blue water on a beach on Union Island in the Grenadines attract many tourists each year.

There are hundreds of islands there, both large and small. Some of the Cayman Islands are no more than tiny strips of sand barely above sea level. Others, like Martinique and Guadeloupe, are made up of several volcanic peaks, and the land area of each island is less than 700 square miles. Cuba, on the other hand, is a huge island. It covers an area of more than 4,300 square miles.

The Gulf of Mexico presents a very different picture. Although it has its share of beautiful coastlines and vacation resorts, many people think of the Gulf of Mexico in terms of oil fields and huge industrial ports. The Gulf is a center for international shipping and home to a huge fishing industry.

Below: The Gulf of Mexico has huge reserves of oil and gas. Offshore oil rigs are a common sight off the Gulf coasts of the United States, Mexico, and Venezuela.

Coastlines and the surrounding large land areas are the most important geographical features in the Gulf of Mexico. Two major rivers, the Mississippi and the Rio Grande, drain into the Gulf, bringing with them freshwater, **sediments**, and sometimes pollution from far inland. The seafloor in the shallower areas of the Gulf contains large stores of oil, gas, and minerals, and the waters are rich with fish and shellfish. The 3,000 miles of shoreline that surround the Gulf are generally low and marshy with many inlets. The Gulf Coast is home to several major international ports.

The Caribbean

The **topography** of the Caribbean seafloor is a complicated pattern of underwater mountain ranges or ridges, deep valleys called trenches, and shallower depressions called basins. There are many basins and trenches throughout the Caribbean, and the sea is dotted with many islands.

The Caribbean is divided into four basins by three underwater ridges. From northwest to southeast, the basins are the Yucatan Basin, the Cayman Trough, the Colombian Basin, and the Venezuelan Basin, and the ridges that separate the basins are the Cayman Ridge, the Nicaragua Rise, and the Beata Ridge.

This complicated structure arose because the Caribbean area is at a place where several of Earth's **plates**, which make up its **crust**, meet. In this area one plate is being pushed below another and an **island arc** is being formed. As a result, other plates are forced to slide past each other to make room.

In the deeper parts of the Caribbean, the seafloor is covered by red clay sediments. On rises, or shallower parts of the seafloor, the sediments are made up of the skeletons of tiny floating plants and animals called **plankton**.

In very shallow areas around the Bahamas, in the northern Caribbean, limestone sediments are being deposited, or laid down. Limestone is a common rock, but most deposits were laid down millions of years ago. The Bahamas are among the few places in the world where limestone is still being laid down today. By studying these deposits, geologists are learning much about how limestones were formed in the past.

Geology in Action

The Caribbean Sea is an excellent place to study the formation of island arcs. Island arcs develop in oceans and seas where one plate shifts below another. The area where the plates dive down is marked by a deep trench. An island arc is forming in the eastern Caribbean today as the North and South American plates slowly dive below the Caribbean plate. The plates meet in an area of deep water to the east of the Antilles called the Puerto Rico Trench. The curved chain of the Greater and Lesser Antilles forms part of the island arc. The active volcanoes in this region show that the arc is still being formed.

Left: *Hot, nearly solid, lava causes steam to rise from the water of the lake formed in a volcanic crater. This active volcano is on the island of St. Vincent and is part of the island arc.*

Below: *Tourists lying in the sun on Cable Beach in Nassau in the Bahamas. The white sands are made up of limestone from the broken calcareous shells of marine animals.*

THE OCEAN FLOOR
The Gulf of Mexico

The Gulf of Mexico has land on three sides, and, unlike the Caribbean, the water is very shallow. Except for the Florida Keys, there are few islands in the Gulf of Mexico. The seafloor topography of the Gulf of Mexico is fairly simple—it is like a bowl-shaped basin with its deepest point in the center. The coastline of the Gulf is interrupted by inlets and **lagoons**. Several large rivers also flow into the Gulf. The rivers carry sand and **silt.** When they enter the Gulf these sediments are deposited and help to form **deltas**, triangular pieces of low-lying land. One of the largest deltas in the world—the Mississippi Delta—is still growing where the Mississippi River enters the Gulf of Mexico near New Orleans, Louisiana.

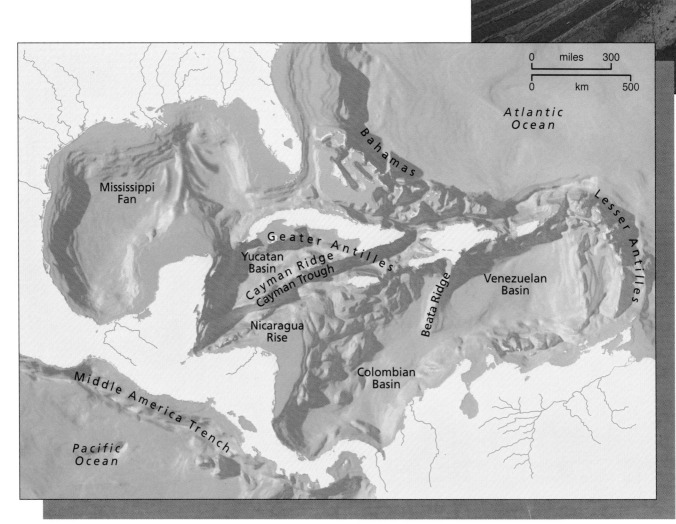

Left: The Mississippi River drains into the Gulf of Mexico, where it forms a delta. The growing Delta extends more than 300 feet farther into the Gulf of Mexico each year.

Left: If all the water were drained from the Caribbean and the Gulf of Mexico, this is how the region would look, with mountain ranges, ridges, and deep basins.

Beyond the coastal area lies a gently sloping zone called the **continental shelf**. This forms a 25- to 200-mile-wide step around the coast and extends to a depth of around 650 feet. Over millions of years, particles of sand, silt, clay, and limestone were deposited on the shelf and on the more steeply dipping area of the **continental slope** beyond. These buried sediments now contain important deposits of oil and gas. Today, the shallow areas of the seafloor near the coast are being covered with sediments washed in from the land, while the deeper areas are being covered by sediments made up of the remains of plankton.

Layers of salt were also deposited a long time ago. These must have formed as seawater **evaporated** from a very shallow basin. This suggests that the sea in the Gulf of Mexico was once much shallower than it is today. The salt layers have been pushed up into large, strangely shaped domes by the weight of the sediments deposited on top of them. Many oil, gas, and mineral deposits are found near the domes on the continental shelf and slope. Salt domes have also been pushed up in some places in the **abyssal plain**.

THE OCEAN FLOOR
Explaining the Differences

Why is the seafloor of the Gulf of Mexico so different from that of the Caribbean? Plate tectonics—the theory that the plates that form Earth's crust move—provides many of the answers. Plate tectonics helps to explain the differences in seafloor topography and why volcanic islands are common in the Caribbean region but not in the Gulf of Mexico. It also helps to explain why valuable natural resources such as oil, gas, and minerals are found in some parts of the region but not in others.

Earth's crust is made up of seven major plates and several smaller ones. Hot, soft rock from inside Earth, called the **mantle**, wells up and pushes the plates around.

How big and how deep?		
	Caribbean Sea	Gulf of Mexico
Area	1,049,500 sq.miles	993,200 sq. miles
Average water depth	7,800 feet	5,000 feet
Maximum water depth	24,720 feet	12,245 feet

When plates meet they can move past each other sideways, they can crash into each other, or, as is happening in the Caribbean, one plate can dive beneath the other. The area where the plate dives down is marked by a deep trench. As the plate dives down toward the center of Earth, it is heated up. Melted rock rises up to the surface again to form a curved string of volcanic islands called an island arc. This plate motion can also cause earthquakes. In the Caribbean, the zone where the plate is diving down is marked by the Puerto Rico Trench, an area of deep water to the east of the Antilles. Islands such as St. Vincent, Martinique, Guadeloupe, St. Lucia, Dominica, and the Grenadines are part of this island arc.

Plate boundaries sometimes occur near the edge of an ocean—but not all shorelines are plate boundaries. For example, the Gulf of Mexico formed in a depression, or low area, in the middle of a plate. In other places, such as the middle of the Atlantic, two plates are moving apart gradually, and new crust is being formed. This new crust is called a spreading ridge.

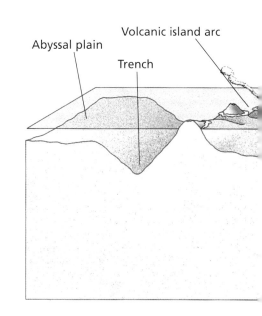

Abyssal plain

Volcanic island arc

Trench

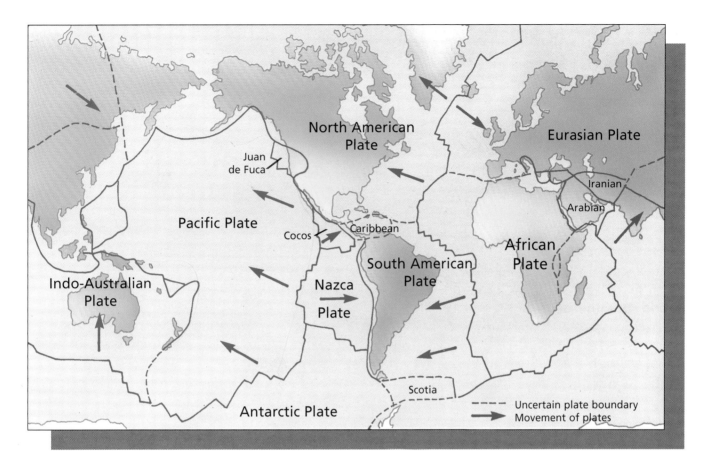

Above: *This map shows the main plates that form the crust, or hard outer layers, of Earth.*

Below: *This diagram shows some of the features of the ocean floor. Trenches and island arcs are formed when one plate dives below another. As the plate sinks it begins to melt. Some of the melted rock, or magma, rises to the surface to form an island arc. A spreading ridge forms when molten rock pushes up and splits apart the oceanic crust. The inset diagram shows details of the ridge. A central rift valley sits between raised, tilted blocks of crust. The valley and the raised blocks are cut across by cracks called transverse faults.*

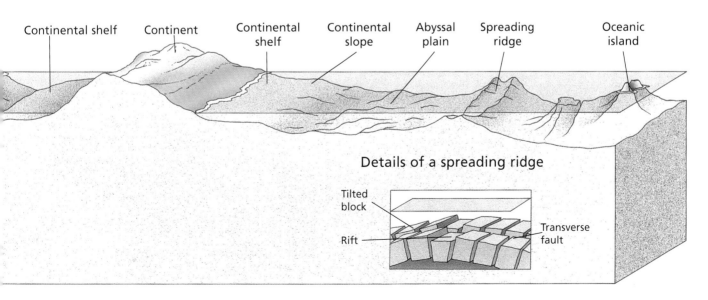

Currents

Ocean water is constantly on the move. Although the surface of the sea throughout the Caribbean and Gulf of Mexico may look similar, it is easy to tell the difference between the water from different areas.

The different bodies of water flow like huge, underwater rivers in a regular pattern of currents. Surface currents are driven by the winds. They carry water from one part of the world to another.

In the Caribbean and the Gulf of Mexico, only the surface waters circulate and mix. There is not much water movement at depths of more than 4,000 feet. However, some colder, deeper water in the Atlantic enters the Caribbean through the few **straits**, such as the Windward, Anegada, and Dominica passages, which are more than 3,300 feet deep.

The Gulf Stream

The Gulf Stream is one of the biggest currents in the world. It is a current of warm water that flows up the east coast of North America, then crosses the Atlantic, carrying warm water to the coasts of Great Britain, Norway, and other European countries. The warm water of the Gulf Stream affects the climate of the land areas it passes. As a result of the Gulf Stream, countries such as Great Britain, Ireland, and Norway have relatively mild winters, even though they are located far north.

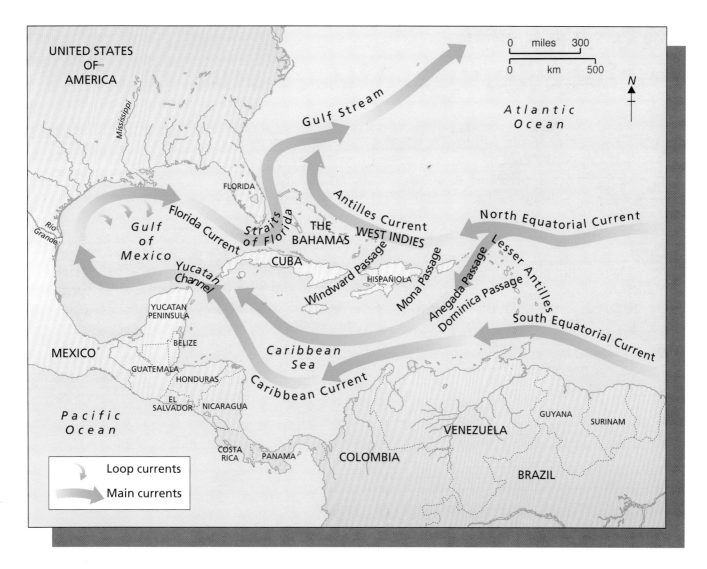

Above: The currents and circulation patterns in the Caribbean and the Gulf of Mexico. The main passages and straits are also shown.

Left: Divers can monitor current flow beneath the surface by using colored dye and watching the direction in which it moves.

Nearer the surface, water from the North and South Equatorial Currents in the Atlantic comes into the Caribbean between the islands of the Lesser Antilles. Once in the Caribbean, the water moves toward the coast of Central America as part of the Caribbean Current. Water from the Caribbean Current pours into the Gulf of Mexico through the Yucatan Channel between Cuba and Mexico, and it flows out into the Atlantic Ocean through the Straits of Florida. As the water reaches the Straits of Florida, the flow becomes very strong and fast and is called the Florida Current.

Some of the water from the equatorial currents also travels east of the Caribbean islands, where it becomes known as the Antilles Current. North of the Bahamas, after it passes out of the Gulf of Mexico, the Antilles Current joins the Florida Current. The two currents combine to produce a major current called the Gulf Stream.

Surface Temperatures and Salinity

Not all seawater is the same: some waters are saltier and some waters are colder. The characteristics of the water also change with depth. For example, colder and saltier waters are more dense and are found toward the bottom of the sea.

In both the Gulf of Mexico and the Caribbean, the surface waters are much warmer than the deep water. In both seas the salinity, or amount of salt in the water, is generally like that in the North Atlantic.

But there are variations. The water is slightly less salty in the northern part of the Caribbean, because of freshwater running off the islands. The Gulf of Mexico also has areas of lower salinity. In general, the water in the Gulf of Mexico is slightly saltier than in the Caribbean, but the Gulf of Mexico also has areas of lower salinity. These lower salinities can be recognized as far as 20 to 30 miles from the coast.

Surface water temperatures and salinity		
	Caribbean Sea	Gulf of Mexico
Surface temperatures	74–85°F	65–75°F
Bottom temperatures	40°F	43°F
Salinity (parts per thousand)	35.5 (north) 36 (south)	36

Left: Salinity levels are lower around some coastal areas of the Gulf of Mexico where big rivers such as the Rio Grande drain, bringing in large amounts of freshwater.

Above: Waves whipped up by strong winds break on a beach in Puerto Rico.

Waves

The same winds that blow across the surface of the water to cause the surface currents in the Caribbean and the Gulf of Mexico also make waves. These waves run freely in deep water, but when they reach shallow water, they are slowed down and may break, producing **surf**. In the Caribbean island chain, the waves are biggest on the eastern, or Atlantic, sides of the islands.

In the Gulf of Mexico the maximum wave heights are less than 15 feet, except during storms. During **storm surges**, waves can reach much greater heights. Storm surges occur more frequently along the northern than the southern or western Gulf coasts. This is because storms entering the Gulf generally pass through the Yucatan Channel and travel north where the pressure is low, which results in an increase in sea level.

Tides and Storms

Tidal range, the difference in height between high tide and low tide, is quite small in the Caribbean and the Gulf of Mexico. Many of the islands in the Antilles have a tidal range of just a foot or less. In the Gulf of Mexico the average tidal range is less than two feet. But in some parts of the Caribbean tidal ranges are much greater. For example, in the Bahamas, tides can be as high as three feet. In some places along the coast of South America, ten-foot tides occur.

Hurricane!

The strongest hurricane to hit the western hemisphere in the twentieth century was Hurricane Gilbert in 1988. This storm destroyed large areas in Jamaica and parts of Mexico. It was followed in 1989 by Hurricane Hugo, which swept through the Caribbean islands of Guadeloupe and St. Croix and destroyed over 90 percent of the houses on Montserrat. In 1995, Hurricane Opal devastated parts of Florida along the Gulf Coast. Many people in the area had to be evacuated to escape winds of up to 125 m.p.h.

In the Caribbean and around Florida, there are two high and two low tides every day. In contrast, around most of the Gulf of Mexico there is just one high tide and one low tide.

The Caribbean and Gulf of Mexico have long periods of fair weather. But during the warmer months the moist tropical air over the region becomes unstable, and storms occur.

Left: In 1992 Hurricane Andrew hit the Gulf Coast of the United States. It overturned vehicles on the roads and caused severe damage to property. Hurricane Andrew first struck in the Bahamas with winds up to 120 m.p.h.

Afternoon thunderstorms, which are sometimes very violent, are common over both land and sea.

Hurricanes are also a threat in the Caribbean and in the Gulf of Mexico. The Caribbean rhyme "June too soon; July stand by; September remember; October, all over" reminds people that hurricanes are a real possibility from July to October. There are, on average, eight major storms a year in the Caribbean. In the Gulf of Mexico there are even more. The hurricanes that strike the Caribbean and Gulf of Mexico arise in the Atlantic, where the **trade winds** from the northern and southern hemispheres meet. Hurricanes begin when warm, moist air rises and then condenses, or changes from gas into water, releasing heat. As this cycle continues, the rising air strengthens and eventually begins to spiral. The hurricanes set off at a speed of only around 12 m.p.h. toward the west-northwest, but they soon build up in size and fury. They can extend up to 500 miles across and the winds can reach speeds of more than 100 m.p.h.

Left: Some of the damage caused by Hurricane Gilbert after it swept through the Caribbean and the Gulf of Mexico in 1988

Life in the Depths

In the Caribbean and the Gulf of Mexico, as in all oceans and seas around the world, marine life is concentrated in the shallowest zones of the ocean, where sunlight can reach. This is because all animals depend in some way on plants to provide them with food, and plants need sunlight to grow.

There are four main depth zones in the ocean. Different forms of life occupy each zone. The shallowest zone is the **epipelagic zone**. There sunlight provides light for plants. Many animals also live in this zone because they feed on the plants. Sunlight barely reaches into the deeper **mesopelagic zone**, so plants cannot grow here. Some of the animals living in this zone swim up to the epipelagic zone at night to feed. Deeper down, sunlight does not reach the **bathypelagic** and **abyssopelagic zones**. Most animals down there rely on the scraps of food that fall down from the zones above.

In the clear waters of the Caribbean, the epipelagic zone extends to around 800 feet. But although well-lit, the levels of important minerals such as nitrogen and phosphorus are low compared to other oceans. As a result, smaller numbers of marine plants and animals live in the Caribbean than in other seas and oceans. But the Caribbean does include many different types of habitats, or living places, and is home to a large number of species of animals and plants.

Along the continental shelf surrounding the Gulf of Mexico region, the habitats for plants and animals are very different from those found in the Caribbean. Large rivers such as the Mississippi carry food and minerals to the shallow, sandy seabed. These conditions provide

Below: In the Gulf of Mexico, fish such as this windowpane flounder can be found.

an ideal home for shrimp, crabs, lobsters, oysters, clams, and scallops. The Gulf is one of the largest shrimp fisheries in the world. Farther offshore, the Gulf is also home to huge numbers of fish such as flounder, snapper, mullet, and menhaden.

Below: The waters in the Gulf of Mexico are extemely rich fishing grounds. This shrimp boat in Key West, Florida, will probably come back with a large catch.

Reefs

Among the most interesting habitats are the underwater reefs that form fringes around the shallow waters of many of the Caribbean Islands. Some of the largest reef areas are found around the islands of Cuba and Puerto Rico and along the coast of Haiti. There, reefs may be over 100 miles long.

Corals are the main reef builders. These are tiny animals, called **polyps**, that tend to live in large groups or colonies attached to a surface. They are related to animals such as jellyfish and sea anemones. The polyps' mouths are surrounded by tentacles, which they use to capture small floating animal plankton for food.

Below: Coral reefs are home to many animals, including this blue sea anemone, which feeds by filtering small particles out of the water or by using stinging cells in its tentacles to capture small animals.

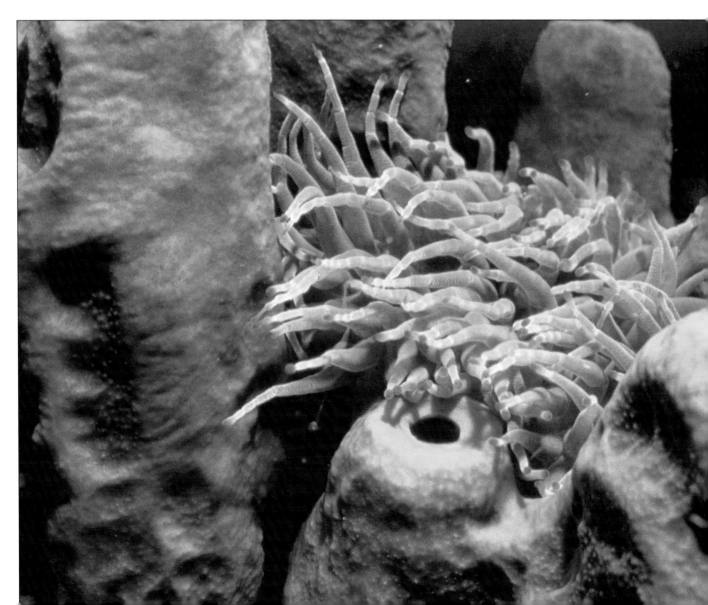

Right: Parrot fish get their name from the beaklike shapes of their mouths. Their teeth are fused together, and they feed by scraping algae and corals from the rocks with their "beaks." They also have teeth in their throats, which grind up the food they have scraped.

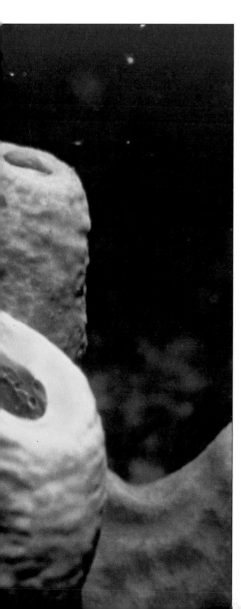

Many corals live together with tiny green plants called algae in a **symbiotic relationship**. The algae live inside the coral and use sunlight to make their own food. The host coral gets some of this food, and in return produces waste products that help the algae grow. Because the algae need sunlight, reef-building corals live only where the water is warm and clear.

Each coral polyp uses minerals dissolved in the seawater to build a limestone skeleton around itself. In some types of corals, the skeletons make large boulders or branching shapes. In other types, individual skeletons are cemented together with lime mud to form a strong wall-like reef. There are about 75 species of corals in the Caribbean, but just 10 of them make up nine-tenths of the reefs.

Because there is plenty of food around the reefs, many other animals live there, including many brightly colored fish. Some, like the damselfish, lay their eggs in the reefs and live by grazing on the algae that live together with the corals. Others, like parrot fish, use their strong jaws to bite off pieces of the reef itself. They crunch it up, spit out the hard limestone framework, and eat the soft coral animals. Some reef fish, such as wrasses, are scavengers that eat dead animals they find on the reef. Hunters, such as groupers, snappers, and barracudas, swim around the reefs and snap at any food that passes by.

Plants and Animals

In some places along the Gulf Coast and along the coasts of some Caribbean islands, fresh water running off the land mixes with seawater in shallow, muddy areas called mangrove swamps. The trees growing in these areas are specially adapted to living in muddy ground often flooded by salt water. They have two types of roots: long, thin roots that dangle from their branches; and long, arching roots that extend above the ground. The arching roots both prop up the trees and trap sediments. This helps the swamp area grow. Mangrove swamps are home to a wide variety of birds, shellfish, snails, insects, and small mammals.

Where Do They Come From?

Although the Caribbean Sea is often thought of as a part of the Atlantic Ocean, many of the animals and plants found there are more like those living in the Indian Ocean and the Western Pacific. This is because ancestors of the marine organisms in the Caribbean today came to the area through the Panama seaway more than four million years ago, before the **isthmus** of Panama rose and separated the two bodies of water.

Five different species of turtles live in the Caribbean. These include the loggerhead, the hawksbill, the ridley, the green turtle, and the leatherback. Leatherbacks are huge reptiles, weighing up to 1,500 pounds, and able to dive to depths of

Below: This leatherback has climbed up on the beach to lay its eggs. The eggs are very fragile, so the turtle covers them with sand to protect them and keep them out of sight.

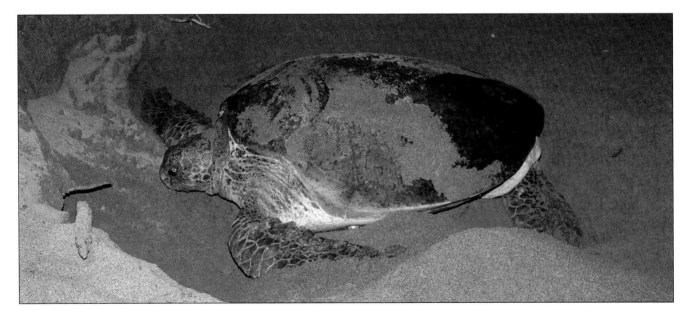

5,000 feet. But although they can live for up to 150 years, their numbers are getting smaller. Now conservation groups are working to protect the leatherbacks from extinction.

Birds, especially waterfowl and shorebirds, flock by the thousands to the shores of the Gulf of Mexico and some of the Caribbean islands. Large colonies of noddies, boobies, pelicans, and other seabirds spend winter along the coasts of Mexico and Cuba and on offshore islands. Migrating birds gather at the mouth of the Mississippi River. This is the start of the Mississippi flyway, an important **migration** route between the birds' winter homes along the Gulf Coast and summer nesting grounds in northern Canada.

The Caribbean and Gulf of Mexico are also home to marine mammals such as sea cows (manatees). Pods of whales and dolphins sometimes swim into the Caribbean from the Atlantic Ocean.

Below: Pelicans, such as this one along the coast of Mexico, feed mainly on fish and other small sea animals.

Settlers

The sea has always been at the center of Caribbean life and still plays an important role today. More than 5,000 years ago, the earliest inhabitants of the Caribbean islands, the Ciboney and Arawak Indians, traveled from South America to the islands by sea. These native people grew crops, fished, and traveled from island to island using canoes made from hollowed-out tree trunks. The word *canoe* comes from the Arawak language.

This peaceful way of life was threatened by the Caribs, a warlike tribe that traveled by canoe from South America and raided the islands in the fourteenth century. Then, in the fifteenth century, explorers from Europe landed on the Caribbean islands—and life for the native peoples there changed forever.

Below: This map shows when various parts of the Caribbean and the Gulf of Mexico region were settled.

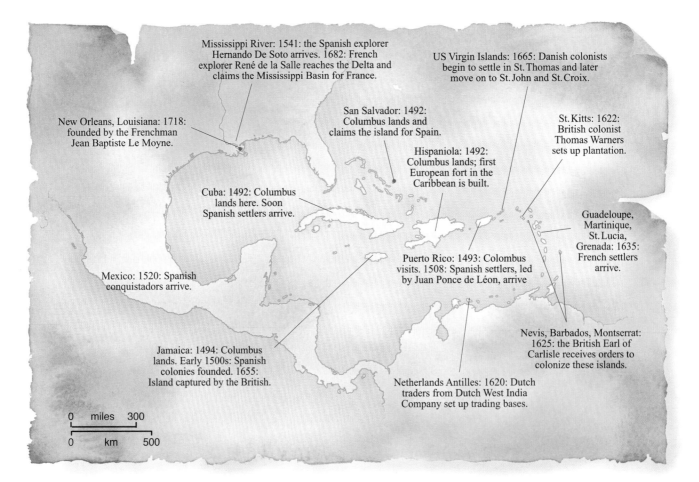

Mississippi River: 1541: the Spanish explorer Hernando De Soto arrives. 1682: French explorer René de la Salle reaches the Delta and claims the Mississippi Basin for France.

US Virgin Islands: 1665: Danish colonists begin to settle in St. Thomas and later move on to St. John and St. Croix.

New Orleans, Louisiana: 1718: founded by the Frenchman Jean Baptiste Le Moyne.

San Salvador: 1492: Columbus lands and claims the island for Spain.

St. Kitts: 1622: British colonist Thomas Warners sets up plantation.

Hispaniola: 1492: Columbus lands; first European fort in the Caribbean is built.

Cuba: 1492: Columbus lands here. Soon Spanish settlers arrive.

Guadeloupe, Martinique, St. Lucia, Grenada: 1635: French settlers arrive.

Mexico: 1520: Spanish conquistadors arrive.

Puerto Rico: 1493: Colombus visits. 1508: Spanish settlers, led by Juan Ponce de Léon, arrive

Jamaica: 1494: Columbus lands. Early 1500s: Spanish colonies founded. 1655: Island captured by the British.

Nevis, Barbados, Montserrat: 1625: the British Earl of Carlisle receives orders to colonize these islands.

Netherlands Antilles: 1620: Dutch traders from Dutch West India Company set up trading bases.

```
0    miles   300
0    km      500
```

The first European explorer to reach the area was Christopher Columbus. While leading an expedition to find a westward route to the riches of the East, Columbus landed on an island in the Bahamas in 1492. He named the island San Salvador and claimed it for Spain. With the help of Arawak guides, he then traveled on to the island of Hispaniola. There one of his ships ran aground. Columbus himself returned to Spain, but he left 40 Spaniards behind to build the first European fort in the Caribbean. Columbus returned to explore the Caribbean and the coasts of Central and South America three more times before his death in 1506.

Although Columbus failed to find the riches he hoped for in the Caribbean, his discovery encouraged many other Europeans to explore the area. The governments of Spain, France, England, Holland (the Netherlands), and Denmark sent explorers to claim islands for themselves, and soon European settlers arrived.

Above This statue in Nassau, the Bahamas, commemorates Christopher Columbus, the first European explorer to reach the Caribbean.

The Colonizers

Dutch traders from the Dutch West India Company began to set up trading bases in the islands of the Netherlands Antilles in the 1620s. In 1635 French settlers came to live in Guadeloupe and Martinique in the French Antilles. In 1665 Danish colonists began to settle in St. Thomas and later moved to St. John and St. Croix in what is now the U.S. Virgin Islands. England and Spain also claimed islands for themselves.

Spanish and French explorers also reached the coast of the Gulf of Mexico. The Spanish laid claim to the lands of Mexico and Central America. But it was the French who eventually took over the coastal land around the mouth of the Mississippi. The city of New Orleans, located on the Mississippi River about 110 miles from the Gulf of Mexico, was founded by Frenchman Jean Baptiste Le Moyne in 1718. It became a vital French stronghold in North America.

The influence of these colonial powers remains very strong today in the language and culture of the Caribbean and Gulf of Mexico areas. A form of French, known as Creole, is still spoken in some areas around the Mississippi Delta. Some of the islands in the Caribbean keep strong links with their colonial past. The islands of Martinique and Guadeloupe are French-speaking and remain overseas departments of France. Dutch is spoken in the Netherlands Antilles, and the islands are still not completely independent from the Netherlands. And Spanish heritage is very obvious in areas such as Cuba and Puerto Rico.

Out of Africa

Many people in the Caribbean are descended from African peoples. Millions of people were captured and brought from West Africa between 1510 and 1865 to work as slaves on sugar plantations in the Caribbean. They worked and lived under appalling conditions. After a number of revolts, slavery was finally ended in 1886.

Many Caribbean people today take pride in their African heritage. The Rastafarians are one example. They believe that Africans are God's chosen people and that Ethiopia is Zion, or heaven on Earth. Many Rastafarians wear their hair uncut and uncombed in long, thick dreadlocks. They eat mostly vegetarian foods and usually prefer herbal remedies to Western-style medical treatment.

Left: *A Rastafarian father wearing his hair in dreadlocks*

Below: *The harbor at St. Thomas, U.S. Virgin Islands. St. Thomas was first settled in 1665 by Danish colonists who later moved to St. John and St. Croix, two other islands in the U.S. Virgin Islands.*

PEOPLE AND THE SEA
Providing Jobs

Many people living around the Gulf of Mexico and in the Caribbean today depend on the sea in one way or another for their living.

The rich mixture of cultures makes the Caribbean islands and Gulf Coast interesting places to visit. Tourists, mainly from the United States and Europe, are also drawn to the Caribbean islands and the resorts along the Gulf of Mexico because of the beautiful beaches and coastlines—and they welcome the opportunities for swimming and diving in the warm, clear sea. Many tourists travel through the islands on cruise ships or yachts.

Below: Old-fashioned paddle wheelers on the Mississippi River add to the atmosphere in New Orleans. The city is both an important port and a tourist attraction.

The tourist industry in the region provides a real boost for local people. It is now the single most important source of income for most of the Caribbean countries. Many local people work in the tourist industry—in hotels, restaurants, shops, airports, and on tourist buses. But careful planning is needed to ensure that the tourist industry does not spoil the area. If the beaches are crowded or dirty and the sea is polluted, tourists will stop coming.

For some local people fishing offers an important source of food and money. For others the sea provides an important trade and transportation route.

Many cities along the Gulf Coast and most of the major towns and cities in the Caribbean are ports. Port cities are the important business and trading centers in the region. Ports provide jobs for local people and are a valuable source of income to the region. Some of these cities, such as Port of Spain in Trinidad, Havana in Cuba, and New Orleans in Louisiana, are centers of international trade. Others, such as Veracruz, Mexico and Mobile, Alabama act as important gateways to business and industrial centers that lie farther inland.

Below: Some tourists enjoy Caribbean vacations by cruise ship. This cruise ship, which is anchored off George Town in the Cayman Islands, is like a floating luxury hotel.

Like elsewhere in the region, port cities reflect their colonial history. In New Orleans the French influence is very noticeable. The old part of New Orleans, called the French Quarter, is where jazz music began, and well-known musicians such as Louis Armstrong rose to fame here. The area is also famous for its Cajun–French-style cooking.

Five Louisiana ports are in the top twelve busiest United States ports in terms of their total amount of shipping and in numbers of tons and value of their exports. The Louisiana ports handle a wide range of cargo, including petroleum, metals, chemicals, grain, and containers. Increased trade between the United

Right: The French influence in New Orleans is clearly shown in the French-style iron balconies of these houses in the French Quarter.

Below: Modern Havana, the capital and major port of Cuba, is a city of skyscrapers. Old Havana, with its narrow alleys and cobbled squares, has kept its Spanish influence.

States and South America means that the Gulf ports are continuing to grow. Another port facility, called Centroport, is being developed on the east side of New Orleans to move some of the New Orleans port's activities away to **wharves** and industrial complexes along the Gulf Coast.

The Spanish influence is clearly felt in Havana, Cuba. The city was settled on the western shore of Havana harbor in 1514. Old Havana, with its narrow alleys, cobbled squares, and eighteenth-century cathedral, has many of the features of an old Spanish city. Large numbers of the old buildings have inner courtyards designed so that the insides of the buildings stay cool.

The port of Havana is a natural harbor surrounded by land. Sugar is the main export handled there. Other exported goods include molasses, citrus fruits, liqueurs, and minerals. The port has berths for all types of ships. These arrive carrying goods such as machinery, fertilizers, oil, and general cargo.

International Shipping

Even with today's air travel, the sea still provides a cheap and efficient way to transport goods and raw materials around the world. The Caribbean nations rely on sea transport to send oil, mineral ores, and other commodities such as sugar, bananas, tobacco, and hardwoods to markets in the United States and Canada. Major ports along the Gulf Coast provide an international gateway for trade between the United States and Mexico.

Both the Gulf of Mexico and the Caribbean Sea provide important international shipping routes. Ships use these seas to reach ports in the southern United States, Mexico, and South American countries. In addition, all ships traveling from the Atlantic to the Pacific oceans via the Panama Canal must sail through the Caribbean.

Ships enter the Caribbean from the Atlantic Ocean, sailing between the islands. The Windward Passage, a channel between Cuba and

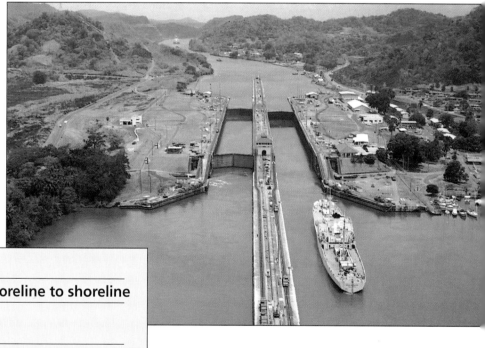

Above: *A ship entering a lock in the Panama Canal. This artificial waterway across the isthmus of Panama connects the Atlantic and the Pacific oceans.*

Panama Canal	
Length	40.3 miles from shoreline to shoreline
Maximum width	300 feet
Minimum depth	41 feet
Number of locks	6 pairs with concrete chambers 1,000 feet long and 110 feet wide
Atlantic Terminus	Cristobal, Panama
Pacific Terminus	Balboa, Panama

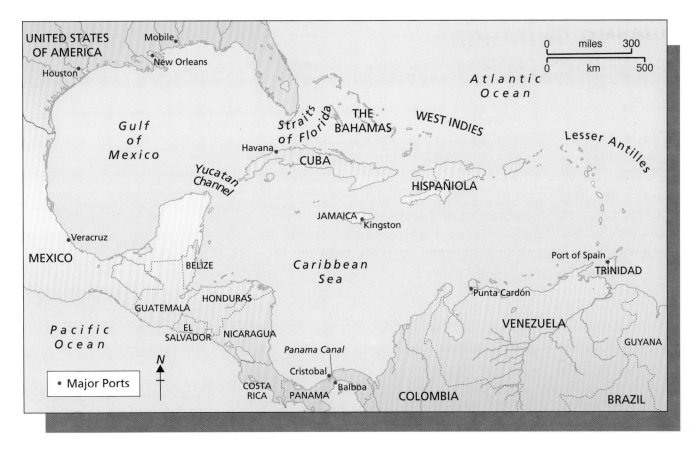

Above: The Gulf of Mexico and the Caribbean are important seas for international shipping. The major ports are shown on this map.

Haiti, is the most important entrance into the Caribbean. Other channels used by international shipping include the Mona Passage, between the Dominican Republic and Puerto Rico and the Straits of Florida, which separate the United States from Cuba and the Bahamas. Once in the Caribbean Sea, navigation is fairly simple.

The Panama Canal is an artificial waterway across the isthmus of Panama in Central America. It connects the Atlantic and the Pacific oceans and shortens the trip from the Atlantic to the Pacific by 7,000 miles. Ships traveling through the Canal pass through six pairs of locks. These locks raise the ships by 85 feet at the beginning of their crossing and lower them by the same amount at the end. Crossing the canal takes just seven to eight hours. Sailing around the tip of South America to reach the Pacific would take many days.

The canal, which is jointly operated by the United States and Panama, was first opened in 1914. It was a commercial success right from the start. The canal is used by ships more than 12,000 times a year. However, it is too small to accommodate modern bulk **tankers** and supertankers, so in 1992 work began to widen the canal.

From Supertankers to Tourist Travel

The Caribbean and the Gulf of Mexico are transversed by both large and small ships. Supertankers travel through the Caribbean and the Gulf of Mexico transporting crude oil from the offshore fields of the Gulf of Mexico and Lake Maracaibo in Venezuela to refineries and also refined oil to distribution centers. The tankers are so big that it is difficult to bring them into port to unload their cargo, so they unload at single **buoy moorings** outside the ports instead.

These large buoys are anchored in deep water and are connected to shore by underwater pipelines. Oil tankers hook up to the pipelines and pump their cargoes directly to refineries and depots on shore. There are several single buoy moorings near major Gulf ports in Texas and Louisiana. Single buoy moorings are also found off the coasts of Cuba, the Dominican Republic, and Trinidad.

Small ships are common in the Caribbean, too. Small ferries carry freight and people between islands. For tourists, cruising and island-hopping by yacht are popular ways of exploring the islands. Some of the smallest islands in the Caribbean can be reached only by yacht.

In 1992 around nine million tourists arrived in the Caribbean on cruise ships. These floating luxury hotels call at various island ports to allow their passengers to explore the islands for the day. The passengers return to the ship at night.

Above: Huge oil tankers are used to transport crude oil to refineries and to carry the refined products to other ports.

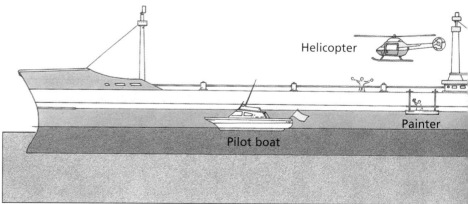

Helicopter

Painter

Pilot boat

Above: This ferry carries people and goods between Port of Spain, the capital of Trinidad, and the neighboring island of Tobago.

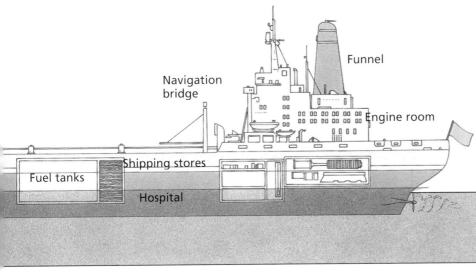

Funnel

Navigation bridge

Engine room

Shipping stores

Fuel tanks

Hospital

Left: The engine, the crew's quarters, the control rooms, and the navigation bridge are at the stern (back) of this oil tanker.

Minerals

The sea is an important source of valuable resources throughout the Caribbean and the Gulf of Mexico. Fish, oil, gas, mineral deposits, and even sand and shells from the seabed are just some of the riches now being exploited.

Some of the most common components of the sea and shore—salt, sand, and shells—are valuable for people and industry. Salt is produced in the eastern Bahamas and in Bonaire in the Netherlands Antilles by evaporating seawater. Magnesium is also extracted from seawater along the Gulf Coast of the United States.

Salt from the Sea

To extract salt, seawater is first collected in flooded fields (pans). It is left to evaporate in the sun and the wind to form a more concentrated solution called brine. The brine is then channeled into other pans specially shaped to increase the evaporation effect. The white crystals that form when the water disappears are then collected, cleaned, and stacked in mounds for shipping abroad.

In the Bahamas, sand is pumped up from the seafloor and shipped to markets in the United States. There it is used for manufacturing bricks, cement, lime, and other building materials. Oyster shells collected from shallow waters along

Left: Fish as well as minerals are important resources throughout the Gulf of Mexico and the Caribbean area. Here, fishermen in a harbor on the Yucatan coast of the Gulf of Mexico inspect their catch.

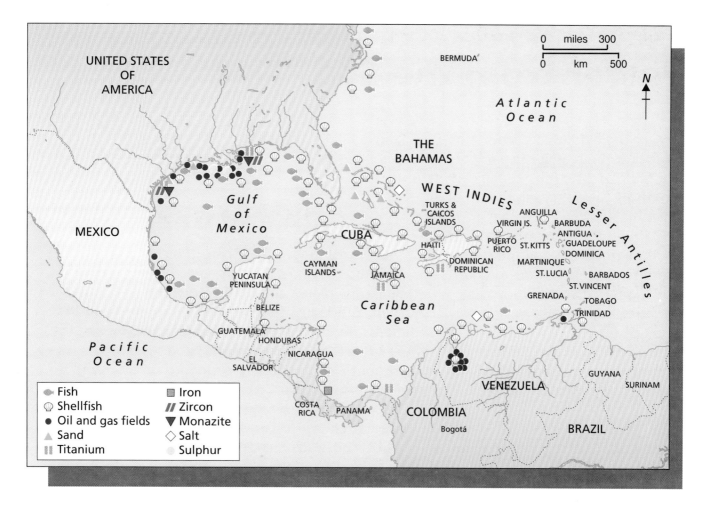

Above: The Caribbean and Gulf of Mexico are an important source of valuable riches. This map shows the locations of the main mineral and hydrocarbon reserves and the major fishing areas.

the Gulf coast of Texas provide material for road building. They are also a valuable source of the mineral calcium carbonate, which is used in the chemical industry.

In some parts of the Gulf of Mexico, minerals deposited in ancient times are now buried below the seafloor, where they form important deposits. In 1960 the world's first offshore sulfur mine began operation in the Gulf of Mexico seven miles off the coast of Louisiana. The sulfur is extracted using the Frasch process, by which very hot water is pumped down boreholes under pressure. The hot water melts the sulfur, which is then pumped out as a liquid.

Many other minerals have also been deposited from ancient seas. In parts of the Gulf of Mexico and in the Caribbean Sea around Costa Rica, Cuba, Haiti, and Colombia, deposits of valuable metals such as titanium, iron, chromite, and gold have been discovered on the seafloor. However, no one has yet found a way to make it worthwhile to mine them.

Power from the Sea

Vast deposits of hydrocarbons (oil and gas) lie buried below the seafloor in parts of the continental shelf of the Gulf of Mexico, especially around the mouth of the Mississippi and along the coast of Mexico. There are also huge reserves of hydrocarbons in the Caribbean in the sediments off the coast of Trinidad and in the Lake Maracaibo area of Venezuela. Hydrocarbons are plentiful in these regions because the geology in these areas provided ideal conditions for their formation.

This "black gold" is a very important source of wealth, especially for countries such as Trinidad and Venezuela. It also makes a large contribution to the world's energy reserves: The oil fields of Lake Maracaibo on the Caribbean coast of Venezuela are some of the most productive in the world.

Oil and Gas

Oil and gas are formed over many millions of years. The process begins when tiny marine plants and animals die and sink to the seafloor. Gradually, they are buried under layers of sediments. As the weight of the sediments grows, the temperature and pressure rise. This causes the organisms to be chemically changed, or "cooked," to form oil and gas. The hydrocarbons form in the tiny spaces, or pores, between grains of a reservoir rock, such as a sandstone. The reservoir rock folds into a dome shape and gets covered with a layer of **impermeable** rock, which seals in the hydrocarbons.

In the Caribbean the seawater itself has the potential to help meet the world's energy needs by helping to power electricity generators. There are two possibilities being studied. One is to use the steady waves on the eastern side of some of the Caribbean islands in wave-power generators to produce electricity.

Another idea is to take advantage of the large temperature difference between the warm surface water in the Caribbean and the much colder bottom water to drive Ocean Thermal Energy Conversion (OTEC) devices. In these devices, liquid ammonia is **vaporized** by the warm surface waters. The vapor, or gas, is used to drive a turbine to generate electricity. It is then cooled and condensed back into a liquid using cold water from the deep

Oil Reserves	
	Estimated reserves (barrels)
Gulf of Mexico	1 billion
Lake Maracaibo	5 billion
Trinidad	1.7 billion

Above: *An Amoco oil platform at Galeota Point, Trinidad. Oil is a very important resource in this region.*

Right: *Waste gas burning off on an onshore oil well in Mexico*

ocean. The electricity produced would be brought to land through cables on the ocean floor.

However, current versions of these devices are not economically feasible. Generating electricity from the Caribbean in this way will have to remain a goal for the future.

Fishing

The relatively shallow and nutrient-rich waters over the broad continental shelf surrounding the Gulf of Mexico are so rich in fish and shellfish that the area is sometimes called the Fertile Fish Crescent. Here, commercial fishing (large-scale fishing for money, not for food) is a major industry. Shrimp, flounder, snapper, mullet, oysters, and crabs are caught in huge numbers. Most of these fish are eaten fresh, although some are smoked or dried. In addition, huge numbers of a fish called menhaden are caught. These are processed into fish meal for use in animal foods. Large carrier vessels up to 130 feet long pump the catch taken by small **seine boats** into their holds and transport them to shore stations.

In contrast, the fisheries in the Caribbean are so poor that most Caribbean countries have to import fish. This is largely due to natural causes. In the Caribbean, as in most tropical seas, there are many different species of fish, but relatively few of each type. In addition, compared to the Gulf Coast, fewer nutrients wash into the sea from the land areas.

Below: Much of the fish caught in the Gulf of Mexico is eaten fresh, but some is smoked and dried. Here, a vendor in a market along the coast of Central America offers dried local fish for sale.

Above: Fresh local fish on a fishing boat in Tobago. Most of the fish caught in the Caribbean are eaten by local people.

Not only are there fewer fish in the Caribbean, but those that are available are more difficult to catch because much of the continental shelf around the Caribbean islands is rough and not suitable for fishing by large trawlers. The coral reefs that surround many of the islands also make navigation difficult for large commercial boats.

Nevertheless, many people in the Caribbean make their living from fishing. The only Caribbean country that has a modern fishing fleet is Cuba. But thousands of local fishermen from other islands fish on the reefs and banks using small craft such as canoes and rowboats with outboard motors. The small fishermen usually sell their catch to fishermen's **cooperatives** and local merchants. The Cuban fishing fleet concentrates on catching shrimp, lobster, and fish such as tuna and mackerel.

Pollution

For much of the Gulf of Mexico and Caribbean Sea, the greatest problems are caused by the growing number of people who live around their long coastlines. As the population grows, so do the amounts of trash, sewage, and industrial waste. If this waste is not properly disposed of, it could pollute the seas and spoil the coastlines.

Not only would this be unpleasant, it could also kill fish and seabirds and cause health problems for people living near the coasts. For the Caribbean islands, which depend more and more on tourism for their livelihood, dirty beaches covered with litter and polluted seas would drive visitors away and spell economic disaster for the region.

Ixtoc 1

On June 8, 1979, drillers working on the Ixtoc 1 well in the Gulf of Mexico faced an emergency. As they drilled into the seabed, oil and gas trapped in the rocks began bubbling up the drill pipe. Soon the flow was out of control. A tremendous explosion followed, and the well blew out. The result was one of the world's largest oil spills: Nearly 140 million gallons of crude oil poured into the open sea. Winds and currents pushed the oil away from the coast, and the slick was broken up in the Gulf, but often oil spills reach the coastline, where they cause great damage.

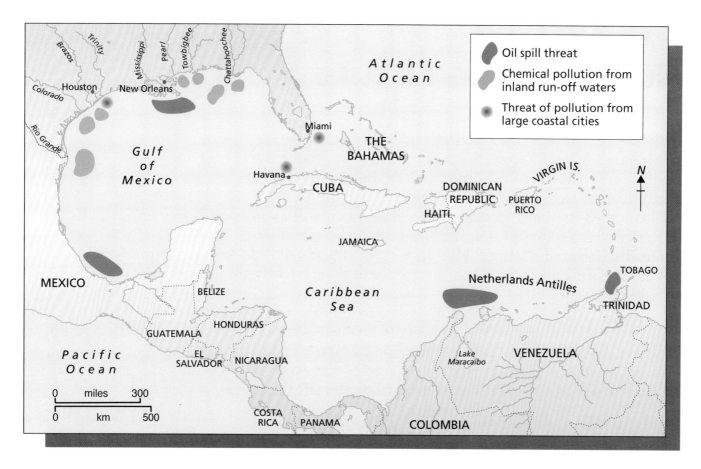

Oil spill threat

Chemical pollution from inland run-off waters

Threat of pollution from large coastal cities

Atlantic Ocean

Houston
New Orleans
Colorado
Rio Grande
Brazos
Trinity
Mississippi
Pearl
Towbigbee
Chattahoochee

Miami

Gulf of Mexico

Havana
CUBA

THE BAHAMAS

DOMINICAN REPUBLIC
HAITI
PUERTO RICO
VIRGIN IS.

N

JAMAICA

Netherlands Antilles
TOBAGO
TRINIDAD

MEXICO

BELIZE

Caribbean Sea

HONDURAS
GUATEMALA
EL SALVADOR
NICARAGUA

Lake Maracaibo
VENEZUELA

Pacific Ocean

0 miles 300
0 km 500

COSTA RICA
PANAMA
COLOMBIA

Above: A growing population and an increase in industrial activities mean that pollution could become a serious problem in the Gulf of Mexico and Caribbean regions. This map highlights the areas most in danger.

The pollution threat is greatest in the Gulf of Mexico because the rivers draining into the Gulf carry with them pollutants from far inland. These include chemicals such as **pesticides**, **herbicides**, and fertilizers that are used on farms far from the coastlines.

Farmers use pesticides and herbicides to kill insects and weeds that damage their crops. But when traces of these substances reach the Gulf, they can also poison the sea life. Fertilizers, which farmers use to help their crops grow better, contain chemicals such as phosphates and nitrogen. When these substances wash into the Gulf they cause the tiny marine plants called algae to grow and reproduce very quickly. The large numbers of algae block out light and reduce the levels of oxygen in the water, especially at night. As a result, fish and other sea life die.

Left: The Ixtoc 1 underwater oil well blowout. The spread of the oil pollution was limited by burning the oil on the surface of the water.

As people look for more ways to make the most of the ocean's resources, the risk of damage to the environment grows. For example, as drilling increases in the oil fields of the Gulf of Mexico, Venezuela, and Trinidad, so does the risk of oil spills. These can spoil beaches and kill sea and bird life.

SAVING THE SEAS
Hope for the Future

It is also important to consider carefully how to preserve the living resources of the sea. Caribbean fishermen would like to be able to take more fish from the sea. But if lots of new fishing boats enter the area, or fishermen begin to use more sophisticated methods to make it possible to catch larger numbers of fish more quickly, the size of the fish population will gradually drop. If too many fish are caught, there will be fewer fish left to reproduce, and eventually the fish populations will die off.

But there are ways to improve the situation. People working together can do a lot to control pollution and protect the resources of the seas. It is not too late to save these resources, and governments are already making a start.

Below: Plastic garbage lasts a long time in the oceans. Plastic dumped from ships can wash ashore, where it litters and spoils beaches.

In 1973 representatives from many countries met to set up the International Convention for Prevention of Pollution from Ships. Then, in 1982, representatives from around the world signed the Law of the Sea Convention, negotiated by the United Nations. The convention sets rules to help protect the ocean environment. Although the convention is not yet fully in force, many countries are already beginning to observe these rules.

As people work to understand more about the oceans and learn how to manage their resources more sensibly, let us hope that we can undo some of the damage of the past and prevent damage in the future.

Above: This car, dumped on St. John's, Antigua, will be rusting away for a long time. If people disposed of their garbage responsibly, the seas and oceans will soon become cleaner environments.

Glossary

abyssal plain The flat and muddy deep seafloor found beyond a continental slope.

abyssopelagic zone The areas of the ocean over 13,000 feet deep. It is extremely cold and dark and few animals live there.

bathypelagic zone The areas of the ocean between about 6,000 and 13,000 feet deep. It is cold and dark and few animals live there.

buoy moorings Large floats anchored to the seabed. They are usually some distance offshore and are often used by ships that are too large to come into a harbor.

continental shelf The land under relatively shallow seas bordering a continent.

continental slope The slope leading down from the continental shelf toward deeper areas of the seabed.

cooperatives Businesses where groups of people band together to buy and sell their goods.

crust The outer layer of Earth's surface.

deltas Triangular-shaped areas of land along some coasts; they extend into the sea from the mouths of rivers.

epipelagic zone The shallowest ocean zone. It extends to depths of about 800 feet. Sunlight reaches this zone and many plants and animals live there.

evaporated Turned from a liquid into gas, often leaving behind dry crystals.

herbicides Chemicals used to kill weeds and other unwanted plants.

impermeable A layer that does not allow liquids or gases to pass through.

island arc A curved string of volcanic islands that sometimes forms when one plate sinks below another.

isthmus A narrow piece of land connecting two larger pieces of land.

lagoons Areas where salt water is separated from the sea by low sandbanks.

mantle The zone between Earth's crust and Earth's core. It extends 1,800 miles beneath Earth's surface.

mesopelagic zone The zone of the ocean between 800 and 6,000 feet deep. Sunlight barely reaches into the top of this zone, and animals that live there must swim up to the epipelagic zone to feed.

migration A journey made by some birds, fish, and other animals at certain times of the year.

pesticides Chemicals that kill animal pests such as insects.

plankton Microscopic plants and animals that drift around in the oceans' surface waters.

plate boundaries The areas where two or more plates meet.

plates The slabs of rock that make up Earth's crust.

polyps Individual coral animals that feed on plankton.

reefs Rigid structures of limestone built by groups of coral polyps living together.

sediments Small particles of sand, mud, silt, or limestone.

seine boats Fishing boats that use weighed-down vertical nets to catch fish.

silt A type of sediment particle that is smaller than sand but larger than mud.

storm surges A piling up of water against the shore caused by high winds pushing the sea's surface during a storm.

straits Sea passages between two land areas.

surf Foam and moving water formed when waves break.

symbiotic relationship A relationship in which two different organisms live together and benefit from each other.

tankers Large ships designed to carry liquid cargo.

topography The shape of a surface. Seafloor topography is the underwater landscape.

trade winds Winds that blow steadily from the subtropics toward the equator.

vaporized Turned from a liquid into a gas.

wharves Platforms used for loading and unloading ships in harbors.

Further Information

FURTHER READING

Calman, Bobbie. *Mexico—The Land*. Lands, Peoples, and Cultures. New York: Crabtree Publishing Company, 1993.

Greenberg, Keith. *Hurricanes and Tornadoes*. When Disaster Strikes. New York: 21st Century Books, 1994.

Hull, Robert. *Caribbean Stories*. Tales from around the World. New York: Thomson Learning, 1994.

Lambert, David. *Seas and Oceans*. New View. Milwaukee: Raintree Steck-Vaughn, 1994.

Mayer, T. W. *The Caribbean and Its People*. People and Places. New York: Thomson Learning, 1995.

Morgan, Nina. *The Mississippi*. Rivers of the World. Milwaukee: Raintree Steck-Vaughn, 1993.

Springer, Eintou Pearl. *The Caribbean*. Revised edition. Silver Burdett Countries. New York: Silver Burdett Press, 1987.

FOR OLDER READERS

Bramwell, Martyn, editor. *Atlas of the Oceans*. Avenel, NJ: Random House Value, 1990.

Fodor's Caribbean. A tourist guide published annually. New York: Fodor's Travel Publications.

CD-ROM

Geopedia: The Multimedia Geography CD-Rom. Chicago: Encyclopedia Brittanica.

USEFUL ADDRESSES

Caribbean Tourism Organization, 20 East 46th Street, New York, NY 10017

Center for Environmental Education, Center for Marine Conservation, 1725 De Sales Street NW, Suite 500, Washington, DC 20036

Earthwatch Headquarters, 680 Mount Auburn Street, P.O. Box 403, Watertown, MA 02272-9104

Index